NATIONAL PARKS
COLORING BOOK

NATIONAL PARKS
COLORING BOOK

Peter F. Copeland

DOVER PUBLICATIONS, INC.

NEW YORK

Map resources for pages 8 and 9 from National Park Services, U.S. Department of the Interior.

Bibliographical Note

National Parks Coloring Book is a new work, first published by
Dover Pubications, Inc., in 1993.

International Standard Book Number

ISBN-13: 978-0-486-27832-2
ISBN-10: 0-486-27832-8

Manufactured in the United States by Courier Corporation
27832815   2014
www.doverpublications.com

Our National Parks

The United States National Park System consists of 357 sites, including historic sites, national monuments and national parks. The system covers more than 80 million acres in 49 states, the District of Columbia, American Samoa, Guam, Puerto Rico and the United States Virgin Islands. Sixteen different types of designated areas lie under the jurisdiction of the National Park Service, which was established in 1916, but this book will be concerned with the national parks.

The Congress established Yellowstone National Park, our first national park, in 1872, beginning a worldwide national park movement. Today more than 100 nations contain some 1,200 national parks or preserves.

Many of our parks preserve archaeological sites commemorating peoples whose history would otherwise have been lost. Others have improved and preserved natural sites and resources. Many rivers, lakes and seashores have been saved from pollution through the efforts of the National Park Service. Most important of all, these parks provide an ongoing learning experience for all Americans, and an example for conservation and preservation efforts in other countries.

In our national parks, uniformed Park Service personnel are available to assist and protect visitors, as well as to instruct them in the recognition and preservation of the parks' many varieties of flora and fauna. These dedicated people give talks, lead hikes, assign campsites and issue warnings about fire hazards and feeding wild animals. They are often called upon to rescue visitors who become lost. The Park Service personnel play a large part in the preservation and maintenance of the parks for future generations of Americans.

In the present book, all 51 national parks (the total number existing in 1993) appear in alphabetical order by their official names, except the Grand Canyon National Park, which appears out of order on the center spread and the Dry Tortugas National Park, which appears on page 61.

Voyageurs NP

Isle Royale NP

MINNESOTA

WISCONSIN

MICHIGAN

IOWA

ILLINOIS

INDIANA

OHIO

MISSOURI

KENTUCKY

Mammoth Cave NP

Great Smoky Mountains NP

TENNESSEE

ARKANSAS

Hot Springs NP

MISSISSIPPI

ALABAMA

GEORGIA

LOUISIANA

MAINE

Acadia NP

VT

NH

NEW YORK

MASS.

CONN.

PENNSYLVANIA

NJ

MD

DE

WEST VIRGINIA

Shenandoah NP

VIRGINIA

NORTH CAROLINA

SOUTH CAROLINA

ATLANTIC OCEAN

FLORIDA

Biscayne NP

Everglades NP

Dry Tortugas NP

Virgin Islands NP

Charlotte Amalie

VIRGIN ISLANDS

Acadia National Park, Maine. Acadia National Park was founded in 1919. With over 41,000 acres, the park preserves the natural beauty of the rockbound coast of Maine, its forests, mountains and offshore islands. Here we see herring gulls passing picturesque Bass Harbor lighthouse at the entrance to Blue Hill Bay. Tourist activities here include boating, swimming, fishing and, in winter, skiing and snowmobiling.

Arches National Park, Utah. Founded in 1971, Arches National Park is located on over 70,000 acres of Utah's dry, stony canyon country. The giant stone arches, windows and spires—the products of the wind and water erosion of over 100 million years—constantly change color as the sun moves through the sky. Wildlife here includes jackrabbits, golden eagles, mountain bluebirds and red-tailed hawks. Here we see a young white-tailed deer viewing one of the great arches in Salt Creek Canyon.

Badlands National Park, South Dakota. The fantastic landscape of the badlands in this national park has been carved by the rain and wind of centuries. Though it may appear barren, this dry and dusty environment supports a host of wild creatures, including buffalo, jackrabbits and coyotes. For many centuries these lands were the home of various Native American tribes. This park was established in 1978 and covers over 240,000 acres.

Big Bend National Park, Texas. Established in 1935, Big Bend National Park extends over 800,000 acres and is located on the great bend of the Rio Grande River on the Mexican border. The river is a winding oasis meandering through the dry West Texas desert and cutting through the Chisos Mountains, a host to myriad wild creatures who have adapted to this harsh desert environment. The golden eagle soars above the river valleys, and mule deer, mountain lions, snakes and coyotes may be seen here, too. Walking, hiking, horseback riding and bird watching are among the park's tourist activities. Be sure to bring your own water when hiking—this is desert country!

Biscayne National Park, Florida. Clear blue seas, dark green woodlands, a bright subtropic sun and many islands distinguish Biscayne National Park, the northernmost coral reef in the United States. Glass-bottomed boats tour the bays and reefs, and scuba diving and snorkeling facilities are available as well. Founded in 1980, this park is perhaps the loveliest part of the famed Florida Keys and extends over 170,000 acres.

14

Bryce Canyon National Park, Utah. This park, founded in 1924, features innumerable varicolored and fantastic stone pinnacles, spires and knobs. These rock formations, perhaps the most colorful and unusual eroded forms in the world, stand in vast amphitheaters in southern Utah. The prolific wildlife at Bryce Canyon includes mule deer, mountain lions and coyotes. Driving and hiking tours and camping are favorite visitor activities in the park, which spreads over 35,000 acres.

Canyonlands National Park, Utah. This is a wilderness of over 337,000 acres of rocky terrain, a geological wonderland in the heart of the Colorado Plateau. The park, founded in 1964, is pierced by the canyons of the Colorado and the Green rivers. Prehistoric Native American rock art and ruins may be seen here on guided tours by car, horseback, motorboat or canoe.

Capitol Reef National Park, Utah. A giant twisting wrinkle in the earth's surface—the Waterpocket Fold—stretches 100 miles across south central Utah. Founded in 1971, Capitol Reef National Park preserves the Fold and its array of fantastically eroded and colorful cliffs, domes and spires. Golden eagles and bighorn sheep may be seen on guided tours of the 241,904-acre park, which is open year-round.

Carlsbad Caverns National Park, New Mexico. Located on over 46,000 acres, Carlsbad Caverns National Park contains a series of connected caverns featuring one of the world's largest underground caves. The park, founded in 1930, contains 76 caves altogether, including the country's deepest, at 1,565 feet. Two tour routes allow visitors to explore the park's underground wonderland.

Channel Islands National Park, California. The five islands that comprise this 249,353-acre park are located off the coast of southern California. Anacapa, San Miguel, Santa Barbara, Santa Cruz and Santa Rosa islands provide homes for nesting seabirds, sea lions—like the one shown here—and a unique variety of plant life. The park, founded in 1980, features abundant marine life as well: giant squid, whales, dolphins, coral and sponges, sea lettuce, sea urchins and abalone. Boaters are warned that rough seas may be encountered around San Miguel Island.

Crater Lake National Park, Oregon. Crater Lake is the center of a collapsed volcano that was gradually filled by rain and melting snow over thousands of years. The lake, 1,932 feet deep, is the deepest in the United States. The park was founded in 1902 and extends over 180,000 acres. Visitors can enjoy boat tours around the lake and a camping area that is open each summer.

Denali National Park, Alaska. Denali, formerly Mount McKinley National Park, was founded in 1917 and covers over 4 million acres. It contains the highest mountain in North America—Mount McKinley. Pictured here, the mountain rises 20,320 feet above sea level. The park is also home to wildlife such as moose, Dall sheep, grizzly bears and timber wolves. Mountain climbing, fishing, camping and airplane tours are among the suggested visitor activities available.

Everglades National Park, Florida. Founded in 1934, Everglades National Park extends over 1.5 million acres. Abundant wildlife, rare and colorful birds, salt-water marshes and mangrove forests distinguish this park, the largest subtropical wilderness remaining in the United States. The shallow waters of Florida Bay are best explored by boat, from which visitors might glimpse sea turtles, porpoises, sharks, alligators and manatees. Bird watching is a popular visitor activity, too. Here we see a Seminole Indian boy poling a dugout canoe through the Everglades.

Gates of the Arctic National Park, Alaska. This park lies entirely north of the Arctic Circle and includes the northernmost extension of the Rocky Mountains. With over 7.5 million acres, it is the second largest of the national parks. Founded in 1980, Gates of the Arctic is a wilderness of jagged peaks, arctic valleys, wild rivers and numerous lakes. Grizzly bears, black bears, wolves, moose, Dall sheep, wolverines, foxes and wapiti (shown here) are among the wildlife living here.

Glacier National Park, Montana. This park, founded in 1910, adjoins Canada's Waterton Lakes National Park. Together they form the Waterton-Glacier International Peace Park, and symbolize the bonds of friendship between our two nations. Over a million acres comprise Glacier National Park, where boating and fishing are popular visitor activities, as are snowshoeing and skiing in wintertime. The mountain goats shown here are more like antelopes than true goats and are related to the chamois of the Swiss Alps.

Glacier Bay National Park, Alaska. This park, extending over 3 million acres, lies west of Juneau and can be reached only by boat or airplane. The sea around Glacier Bay is a wonderworld of whales. Mighty humpback whales, like the one pictured in the foreground, killer whales, which are also called the wolves of the sea, and Minke whales are often seen in these far northern waters that border Canada. Camping, boating and fishing are among the favorite tourist activities in this park, which was established in 1980.

Grand Teton National Park, Wyoming. This park, founded in 1929, is located on over 300,000 acres of one of the most impressive mountain ranges on the North American continent. Grand Teton, the park's highest mountain, is over 13,000 feet above sea level. Bighorn sheep, like the ones shown here, roam the mountains at the park's northern end. Black bear, moose and elk may also be seen here.

Great Basin National Park, Nevada. This park was established in 1986 and extends over 77,000 acres. Its major features include a remnant ice field on 13,000-foot Wheeler Peak, an ancient bristlecone pine forest and Lex- ington Arch, a 75-foot limestone formation. Park rangers lead nature walks and tours through the tunnels and deco- rated galleries of the Lehman Caves. Here we see a golden eagle coming to rest near Wheeler Peak.

Great Smoky Mountains National Park, North Carolina and Tennessee. The Great Smoky Mountains form the loftiest mountain range in the eastern United States. Rich and diversified plant and animal life can be seen in the park, including bobcats, great horned owls, black bears and red foxes. The park was established in 1926 and extends over more than 500,000 acres. Here, an early mountain farm can be seen at the unique Open Air Museum, which shows visitors what life was like for the early mountain settlers.

Guadalupe Mountains National Park, Texas. This park, founded in 1966, preserves the rugged spirit and remote wilderness of America's Old West. On a hike through McKittrick Canyon, you can see the transition from desert to forest. The park spreads over more than 86,000 acres, and its wildlife, including the colorful collared lizard, is typical of the Southwest's forests and deserts.

Haleakala National Park, Hawaii. This national park, extending over 28,000 acres, was founded in 1960. Haleakala crater, on the island of Maui, is now a cool, cone-studded reminder of a once-active volcano. Among other park activities, such as camping and picnicking, park rangers guide tourists on crater-rim walks during the summer months. The visitors shown here are looking down from the crater rim into the heart of the ancient volcano.

Hawaii Volcanoes National Park, Hawaii. This park of over 200,000 acres features some of the active volcanoes on the island of Hawaii. Since 1969, repeated eruptions have created new molten lava flows, or "fountains of fire," from Mauna Ulu, "the growing mountain." The massive sea arch shown here has been carved by wave erosion along the Kalapana coastal section of the park. Hawaii Volcanoes was established as a national park in 1916.

Grand Canyon National Park, Arizona. This park, featuring the world famous Grand Canyon of the Colorado River, is a truly amazing phenomenon of nature. The Canyon is a mi deep gorge, four to 18 miles wide and 217 miles long. Wor

annot express the fantastic landscape where myriad wildlife may be seen, including nighthawks, eagles, bluebirds, bob- cats, mule deer and mountain lions. The park, founded in 1919, consists of over a million acres of spectacular scenery.

Hot Springs National Park, Arkansas. In 1921, the United States government set aside this area—almost 6,000 acres—as a national park. Persons suffering from illnesses and injuries sought relief in the ancient tradition of thermal bathing and by drinking the water of the park's 47 mineral hot springs. In the mid-nineteenth century, the Springs became known as the "National Spa." Here we see the Hot Springs Mountain Tower, which rises high above the Hot Springs National Park area. From the top of the tower, visitors may enjoy a spectacular view of the Ouachita Mountains and the Spa City, Hot Springs.

Isle Royale National Park, Michigan. This park, established in 1931, extends over 570,000 acres along the northwest corner of Lake Superior. A roadless land of wild creatures, unspoiled forests, lakes and rugged shores, the park is accessible only by boat or floatplane. The archipelago is a sanctuary for wild game—moose and wolves, like the ones shown here, beavers, red foxes and a variety of birds and smaller animals.

Katmai National Park, Alaska. Fifteen volcanoes line the Shelikof Strait, making Katmai one of the most active volcano centers in the world. Established in 1980, the park also covers over 3 million acres, and is one of the last refuges of the Alaskan brown bear, the world's largest land carnivore. Other wildlife at Katmai includes moose, caribou, lynx, swans and geese. Floatplanes fly visitors in from Anchorage, especially for the salmon fishing.

36

Kenai Fjords National Park, Alaska. Believed by many to contain over 650,000 acres of the most spectacular landscape in all of Alaska, Kenai Fjords National Park was established in 1980. The east arm of Nuka Bay, shown here as viewed from about 5,000 feet up, reveals the general appearance of the fjords along the park's oceanfront; a rain forest forms another part of the shoreline. The rocky coast provides resting places for seals, sea lions and otters, while the forest is the home of black and brown bears, moose, wolves, wolverines and mink.

Kings Canyon National Park, California. This park was founded in 1940 and covers over 450,000 acres of wilderness. Two giant canyons of the Kings River and the peaks of the High Sierra Mountains dominate the landscape. More than 400 miles long, the Sierra Nevada range exceeds the Alps in area and contains six peaks over 14,000 feet in elevation. Black bears roam the wilderness and occasionally raid tourist camps for food, which can cause some excitement.

Kobuk Valley National Park, Alaska. This park, established in 1980 and made up of over 1.7 million acres, embraces the central valley of the Kobuk River, and lies entirely north of the Arctic Circle. Here, in the northernmost extent of the boreal forest, is a rich array of arctic wildlife, including the largest herd of caribou in North America—over 300,000 animals, like the one seen here. There are also grizzly and black bears, wolves and foxes. Motorboats, kayaks, canoes and rafts are used to explore the Kobuk River.

Lake Clark National Park, Alaska. This park is located on over 2 million acres in the heart of the Chigmit Mountains along the shore of Cooke Inlet in southeast Alaska. Established in 1980, Lake Clark National Park is a land of jagged peaks and granite spires, as well as two active volcanoes and over 20 glacier-carved lakes. Summer visitor activities include backpacking, river running and fishing.

Lassen Volcanic National Park, California. Between 1914 and 1921, there were volcanic eruptions at Lassen Peak, this park's central feature. The park, established in 1916 and covering over 100,000 acres, is a laboratory of volcanic phenomena, with sulphur vents, steaming mud pots and hot springs with waters above 100 degrees centigrade. Fishing at Lassen requires a California permit, and boating is limited to nonpower craft. Camping and hiking are favorite activities at the park, with seven campgrounds available for visitors. A mule deer is illustrated in the foreground.

Mammoth Cave National Park, Kentucky. Mammoth Cave is the centerpiece of one of the greatest cave regions in the world. Established in 1926, the park, with over 50,000 acres, abounds in limestone caves, underground rivers, springs and sinkholes. The intricate labyrinth of Mammoth Cave was carved out by underground water forcing its way through cracks and between layers of rock. Unusual fish, shrimp, crayfish, crickets and spiders live in the cool darkness of the cave. Many are blind, or nearly so, from living their lives in darkness.

Mesa Verde National Park, Colorado. Mesa Verde, established as a park in 1906, features the finest and best preserved pre-Columbian cliff dwellings in the nation. Over 1,000 years ago a group of Native Americans chose this high plateau above the Montezuma and Mancos valleys for their home and built dwellings of sandstone blocks under the overhanging cliffs. There are summertime guided tours and camping programs at Mesa Verde, which extends over 50,000 acres. Three major cliff dwellings on Chapin Mesa are open for visits in season and many others are visible to visitors from Ruins Road.

Mount Rainier National Park, Washington. Established in 1899, this park of over 230,000 acres features the greatest single-peak glacier system in the United States. Its slow-moving rivers of ice radiate from the summit and slopes of Mount Rainier, an ancient volcano. Mountain climbing at this park is suggested only for experienced climbers who are equipped for it. There are tremendous snowfalls and the trails are often not cleared until mid-July.

North Cascades National Park, Washington. This park was founded in 1968. Its wild (and roadless) alpine landscape of lush forests and meadows is a true mountain kingdom of plant and animal life. Nature trails are scattered throughout the park's 500,000 acres, and can be enjoyed in the summer. Cross-country skiing, camping, boating, fishing and hiking are favorite visitor activities.

Olympic National Park, Washington. This mountain wilderness, established as a national park in 1938, contains a remnant of Pacific Northwest rain forest, glaciers, 50 miles of wild scenic ocean shoreline, and the rare Roosevelt elk. At Olympic, which covers over 900,000 acres, fishing, mountain climbing and a variety of winter sports are among featured activities.

Petrified Forest National Park, Arizona. The main features of this park are trees that have petrified, or changed to multicolored stone, as well as Indian ruins and petroglyphs. The park, extending over 90,000 acres, also contains portions of the colorful Painted Desert. Although there are no campgrounds in the park, wilderness backpack camping is allowed. Here we see two visitors filming the trunk of an ancient petrified tree that lived perhaps 225 million years ago. This petrified forest was established as a national park in 1962.

Redwood National Park, California. This park was established in 1968 and has over 100,000 acres. The world's tallest trees grow here, virgin groves of ancient redwoods. The park also includes 40 miles of scenic Pacific coastline. The coastal drive offers breathtaking views of crashing surf and a vast panorama of the Pacific Ocean. Park streams offer fishing for trout, as shown here, and Chinook salmon.

Rocky Mountain National Park, Colorado. The massive grandeur of the Rocky Mountains may be viewed from Trail Ridge Road, which crosses the Continental Divide. Established in 1915, the park features mountain peaks towering more than 14,000 feet above sea level. Wildlife and wildflowers in profusion greet the summer visitor. Horses with guides can be hired at two locations within the park, which covers over 260,000 acres.

Samoa National Park, American Samoa. Samoa National Park is one of the newest of the nation's 51 national parks, established in 1988. The park features the wild scenery of two rain forest preserves. Located in the South Pacific, the park is in three separate areas on separate **islands**, totaling nearly 9,000 acres. Ta'u is the largest island, an undisturbed rain forest. The red cliffs along its south coast are spectacular. There is also a coral reef off the island of Ofu. Visitors to the park can enjoy unique tropical animals and explore the Samoan villages in the area. It is suggested that visitors observe the customs of the native Polynesian people when visiting these villages.

Sequoia National Park, California. This is America's second-oldest national park, created in September 1890 and originally called General Grant National Park. In 1940, its 400,000 acres became part of Kings Canyon National Park. The giant sequoia trees shown here can live to be over 3,000 years old and can grow to over 300 feet in height. Visitors enjoy camping, day hikes and backpacking, but are cautioned to beware of rattlesnakes.

Shenandoah National Park, Virginia. In 1926, almost 200,000 acres of scenic landscape were set aside to form this park. Skyline Drive winds through its fields and forests, along the crest of the Blue Ridge Mountains, provid- ing visitors with spectacular views of the Shenandoah Valley. Deer, bears, bobcats and wild turkeys, as well as the ducks shown here, abound in the rich Virginia countryside.

Theodore Roosevelt National Park, North Dakota.
This park of over 70,000 acres includes scenic badlands along the Little Missouri River as well as a part of Teddy Roosevelt's Elkhorn Ranch. The future president, shown here with a friend, first came to the badlands in 1883 and enjoyed many of the activities available to visitors today. Saddle horses may be rented within the park and picnicking is also permitted. The park, which was established in 1978, is the home of more than 200 species of birds, many of which are songbirds.

Virgin Islands National Park, United States Virgin Islands. Although there are rumors of buried treasure throughout the Virgin Islands, visitors don't have to hunt for the wealth of this park's magnificent beaches, and diverse plant and marine life. With over 14,000 acres, the park's coastal areas also contain mangrove swamps, which form protective nurseries for sea life, and coral reefs, magnificent wildernesses of colors and shapes. Swimming, skin diving, fishing, hiking, boating and sailing are all popular visitor activities at this park, which was established in 1956.

Voyageurs National Park, Minnesota. In 1971, more than 200,000 acres of land were set aside to establish Voyageurs National Park. A region of interconnected northern lakes dotted with islands, the area was once part of the route used by the French-Canadian voyageurs—fur trappers who carried their pelts from the far northwest to Montreal. Wildlife here includes the beaver, shown here building a dam, and wolves. The park lies in the heart of the only region in the continental United States where the eastern timber wolf survives.

Wind Cave National Park, South Dakota. Founded in 1903, there is much more to Wind Cave National Park than its underground geological wonders. A diverse mix of wildlife—prairie dogs, bison and pronghorn (like the ones shown here)—dwells on over 28,000 acres of rolling grasslands. Ranger-guided cave tours are offered several times daily.

Wrangell-St. Elias National Park, Alaska. Three mountain ranges converge here in what is often referred to as the "mountain kingdom of North America." The park, with over 8 million acres, includes the continent's largest system of glaciers and the second highest mountain peak in the United States—Mount St. Elias—at 18,008 feet above sea level. The park, established in 1980, is characterized by remote mountains, valleys and wild rivers, all rich in wildlife. Cross-country skiing is a favorite visitor activity.

Yellowstone National Park, Wyoming, Idaho and Montana. Old Faithful, shown here, and some 10,000 other geysers and hot springs make this the world's most famous geyser area. Over 2 million acres of lakes, water-falls, abundant wildlife, mountain meadows and the Grand Canyon of the Yellowstone form the world's first national park, established in 1872.

Yosemite National Park, California. Granite peaks and domes tower high above meadows in the heart of the Sierra Nevadas; groves of giant sequoia trees dominate the woodlands. Lakes and waterfalls, including the highest in the nation, are found here, too. The park embraces over 760,000 acres of scenic wildlands, set aside in 1890 to preserve a portion of the Sierra Nevada.

Zion National Park, Utah. The massive, multicolored vertical cliffs and deep canyons of Zion present some of the most spectacular scenery in the nation. Guided horseback rides and tram tours through the park's 146,000 acres are available. The park, established in 1919, is also a wildlife sanctuary. It provides a safe environment for mountain lions, golden eagles, roadrunners and other bird life, like the three sharp-tailed grouse, shown here.

Dry Tortugas National Park, Florida. Almost seventy miles west of the Florida Keys lies a cluster of seven coral reefs discovered by Spanish explorer Ponce de León in 1513. These reefs, famous for legends of sunken pirate gold and a variety of bird and marine life, were called the Tortugas for the great number of turtles found there; later, mariners added the word "Dry," to remind sailors that the islands contain no fresh water. Fort Jefferson, the park's central feature, served as a military prison during the Civil War. The fort's most famous prisoner was Dr. Samuel Mudd, the physician who set the broken leg of Lincoln's assassin, John Wilkes Booth. In 1935 President Franklin D. Roosevelt made the area a national monument and in 1992 it was redesignated a national park. Today visitors can enjoy boating, snorkeling and scuba diving in the waters off the Dry Tortugas.